HUNTER
EDUCATION
NIGHTINGALE

YEAR

5

Time *for*
NAPLAN

LITERACY PRACTICE
ACTIVITIES

**Robert
Stanley**

HUNTER
EDUCATION
NIGHTINGALE

Copyright © 2018 Robert Stanley
Time for NAPLAN - Literacy Practice Activities - Year 5

Published by:
Hunter Education Nightingale
ABN: 69 055 798 626
PO Box 547
Warners Bay NSW 2282
Ph: 0417 658 777
email: sales@huntereducation.com.au
website:www.huntereducationnightingale.com.au

Cover Design: Brooke Lewis

National Library of Australia Card No.
and ISBN 978 - 1 - 925787 - 02 - 3

RECYCLING

When the program is completed and the paper no longer wanted, be sure to have it recycled. The time and care taken to recycle may help save a tree and maintain our environment.

Time for NAPLAN
LITERACY PRACTICE ACTIVITIES
YEAR 5

Time for Naplan Literacy Activities Year 5 is the third in a series designed for students to practise the types of activities presented in using and understanding literacy. There are six assessment tests in this book that will help students identify the conventions used in punctuation, rules of spelling and editing along with reading for understanding. Many activities treat aspects of language in the context of reading.

As the student progresses through the assessment tasks he or she becomes familiar with the types of activities used to measure the understanding and application of the topic in the context of language.

The following skills are assessed.

- **Spelling**   - in the context of sentences (correct spelling errors)
  - Knowledge and application of spelling rules
- **Punctuation** - assessing knowledge of varying conventions with punctuation
- **Reading**   - identifying main idea of a story
  - understanding meanings of words in context of the text
  - ability to identify a story's purpose
  - classify the text type as part of reading conventions
- **Writing**   - Following the scaffold outline of a story.
  - Follow conventions - punctuation, sentence structure, correct spelling, paragraphing and use editing skills to make corrections.
- **Language Conventions** - A wholistic approach

Message to Parents

This book will help identify areas where knowledge and understanding of literacy is competent as well as identify areas in need of attention. Use each set of assessment tasks as a tool only. Assist your child when and where necessary. Encourage praise, keeping the process a positive experience. Your support will play a big part in the process of learning while showing you where help is needed.

The spelling mistake in each sentence has been circled. In the box next to each question, write the correct spelling for each circled word.

1. I travelled to the beach with my (famly.)

2. Tom took a picture of his (frends) to put in his photo album.

3. Beetles and bugs are types of (insecs.)

4. Mr Faros was rescued in the (flud.)

5. The King ordered a (serch) for the missing jewels.

6. An (angrey) bull rushed at the bull fighter.

7. Carlo sent the cricket ball crashing (threw) the window.

8. When Minh received her award, Mum and Dad were (prowd.)

The spelling mistakes in these labels have been circled. In the box next to each question, write the correct spelling for each circled word.

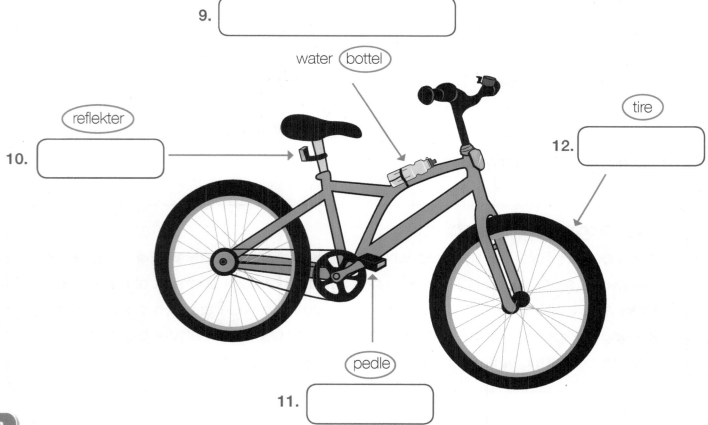

9.

water (bottel)

reflekter

10.

tire

12.

pedle

11.

Each of these sentences has one word that is incorrect. In the box next to each question, write the correct spelling for each circled word.

13. David was given a big (suprise) for his birthday.

14. If an earthquake occurs it will (distroy) many homes.

15. Our class performed a dance at the (consert.)

16. You should (lissen) carefully in class.

Each of these sentences has one word that is incorrect.
In the box next to each question, write the correct spelling for each circled word.

17. The mechanic put a new (moter) in the car.

18. Do you (rember) going to the zoo last year?

19. Tam was wearing a (difrent) jumper today.

20. You may go out to lunch if you (compleat) your work.

21. I will (interduce) you to my new friend.

22. We blew up lots of (ballons) for the party.

23. The building of the new road will (commense) in December.

24. (Sumtimes) I like to go swimming at the pool.

25. It is (dangerus) to play with matches.

Read the text *Getting Fit for Soccer*. Choose the correct words that fill the gaps in the text.

Shade one bubble. 🖉

Getting Fit for Soccer

26. First, Helen jogs around the park so that _____ muscles are warmed up.

- ○ she
- ○ them
- ○ she's
- ○ her

27. The team then practise passing the ball before _____ have a game.

- ○ she
- ○ they
- ○ it
- ○ I

28. _____ has a quick walk around the soccer field to warm down.

- ○ Finally, Helen
- ○ Finally, helen
- ○ finally, Helen
- ○ finally. helen

Shade one bubble. 🖉

29. Which sentence contains the correct punctuation?

- ○ What is the time now in England?
- ○ What an amazing game?
- ○ What beautiful music that was?
- ○ What fun we had on our holiday?

30. Which sentence contains the correct punctuation?

- ○ "May I borrow your pencil?" asked Minh.
- ○ "May I borrow your pencil? asked Minh
- ○ "May I borrow your pencil," asked Minh
- ○ "May I borrow your pencil." asked Minh.

31. Which word makes this sentence make sense?

_____ her head hurt, she continued to play.

- ○ Even
- ○ During
- ○ Before
- ○ Although

Shade two bubbles.

32. Where should the missing speech marks go?

◯ What a fantastic goal! ◯ cried the commentator ◯ who jumped up from his seat. ◯

Shade one bubble.

33. Which word correctly completes the sentence?

After the car accident, the driver was _____.

◯ shook   ◯ shakes   ◯ shaken   ◯ shake

34. Which word correctly completes the sentence?

Yesterday, I _____ the two cars collide and cause the accident.

◯ seen   ◯ see   ◯ sawn   ◯ saw

Read the text The Blue Whale. Choose the correct word to fit in each gap.

Shade one bubble.

The Blue Whale is not only the biggest whale but also the biggest animal in the world. You can

find _____ 35. _____ creatures all over the world. They will usually be found _____ 36. _____

the surface of the ocean living in small groups known as pods.

Blue Whales breathe _____ 37. _____ two blowholes, which can be found at the top of

_____ 38. _____ head. When it blows, a stream of water

can be seen shooting above the surface of the water.

Blue Whales _____ 39. _____ small fish, krill and plankton.

35.	◯ this	◯ these	◯ them	◯ that
36.	◯ in	◯ near	◯ with	◯ of
37.	◯ in	◯ under	◯ for	◯ through
38.	◯ his	◯ its	◯ her	◯ their
39.	◯ eat	◯ ate	◯ eating	◯ are

Read the text Athletics Carnival. Choose the correct word to fit in each gap.

Shade one bubble.

Athletics Carnival

40. As they came around the bend, Mark ran

    very _____. He smiled to

    himself as he felt the wind at his heels.

    ○ quicker
    ○ quickly
    ○ quick
    ○ quickest

41. However, two runners _____ getting

    closer and Mark looked over his shoulder to

    see how far away they were.

    ○ was
    ○ is
    ○ were
    ○ will be

42. Which word makes this sentence correct?

    April _____ her new bag to school to show her friends.

    | buy | bought | bring | brought |
    | ○ | ○ | ○ | ○ |

43. Which word makes this sentence correct?

    _____ turn is it to mop the floor?

    | Whose | Whom | Who's | Which |
    | ○ | ○ | ○ | ○ |

44. Which word or words makes this sentence correct?

    In the car race, Holden had a faster time than Ford, but Mitsubishi was

    _____ of them all.

    | the fastest | the faster | faster | fast |
    | ○ | ○ | ○ | ○ |

PRACTICE 1

Shade one bubble.

45. Which word describes how the child wrote?

     After Sam wrote (neatly) in his book, he walked over to the Library

     and (carefully) chose a (colourful) book to read.

46. Which of these sentences should end in a question mark?

     ⬭ How exciting the holiday will be   ⬭ How beautiful the flowers were

     ⬭ How will you travel to the city   ⬭ How to make a paper plane

47. Which option completes the sentence correctly.

     Mum bought _____ from the shop .

     ⬭ apples, grapes and bananas   ⬭ apples grapes, and bananas

     ⬭ apples, grapes, and, bananas   ⬭ apples grapes and bananas

48. Which word or words makes this sentence correct?

     The game was called off because

     ⬭ is rain falling   ⬭ rain had fallen

     ⬭ rain was fallen   ⬭ rain would fall

49. Where should you place the missing comma?

     After   finishing   her work   Sally raced off   to play netball
       ⬆   ⬆   ⬆   ⬆
       ⬭   ⬭   ⬭   ⬭

50. Which sentence uses the apostrophe (') correctly?

     ⬭ Tony's friends like to play with cricket bats.

     ⬭ Tonys' friends like to play with cricket bats.

     ⬭ Tonys friend's like to play with cricket bats.

     ⬭ Tonys friends like to play with cricket bat's

9

Born to Fly

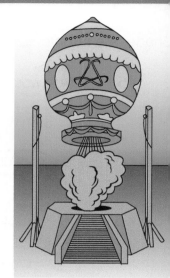

Joseph Montgolfier was born on August 1740 in Annonay, France. His brother Jacques Etienne Montgolfier was born five years later. They invented the first practical hot air balloon.

Joseph often wondered about the clouds and his desire was to fly. After trying many experiments, he managed to make a taffeta envelope with hot air rise to the ceiling.

This small success led to the brothers trying to float bags made of paper and fabric. They found that when they held a flame near the opening at the bottom of the bag it expanded with hot air and floated upward.

The brothers then built a large paper-lined silk balloon. The first demonstrated flight of this hot air balloon took place on June 4, 1783, in Annonay, France. It rose 1,000 metres in the air.

The first passengers in a hot air balloon were a rooster, a sheep and a duck. On September 19, 1783, in front o King Louis XVI, these creatures flew for eight minutes, rose to a height of 500 metres and travelled 3 kilometres in Paris.

The first manned flight took place on October 15, 1783. The first human passengers on a Montgolfie balloon were Pilatre de Rozier and Marquis d'Arlandes. The balloon was in free flight, meaning it was not tethered.

In the city of Lyons, a huge Montgolfier hot air balloon carried seven passengers to a height of 3,000 feet or January 19, 1784.

The brothers thought that they had discovered a new gas (they called Montgolfier gas) that was lighter than air and made the inflated balloons rise. They simply didn't realise that hot air caused balloons to rise.

Read *Born to Fly* on page and answer questions

1. Jacques Etienne Montgolfier was born in

     ○ 1735.   ○ 1740.   ○ 1745.   ○ 1750.

2. Montgolfier gas was really

     ○ Helium.   ○ hot air.   ○ Oxygen.   ○ Argon.

3. "The balloon was in free flight, meaning it was not tethered." Tethered probably means

     ○ heavy.   ○ light.   ○ tied down.   ○ expensive.

4. A hot air balloon flight carrying seven passengers took place in

     ○ Annonay.   ○ Paris.   ○ Lyons.   ○ Bordeaux.

5. The hot air in the balloons was probably provided by

     ○ the wind.   ○ a flame.   ○ gunpowder.   ○ Montgolfier gas.

6. The first passengers in a balloon were

     ○ A goat, a pig and a sheep.   ○ Pilatre de Rozier and Marquis d'Arlandes.

     ○ King Louis XVI.   ○ A rooster, a duck and a sheep.

First Man on the Moon

On May 21 1961, the US President, John F. Kennedy challenged the country to send people to the moon before the end of the decade.

On July 16 1969, the Apollo 11 was launched from the Kennedy Space Centre. Inside Apollo 11 were three astronauts; Neil Armstrong, Edwin (Buzz) Aldrin and Michael Collins.

Four days later, Commander Neil Armstrong became the first man on the moon. As he descended the Lunar Module and stepped out onto the moon he said the famous words: "One small step for man, one giant leap for mankind."

The astronauts needed to wear space suits with a portable life support system on their backs to walk on the surface of the moon. This system gave the astronaut oxygen to breathe and it controlled the temperature and pressure inside the suit.

There was less gravity on the moon so the astronauts could jump very high in comparison to jumping on Earth.

Armstrong and Aldrin spent a total of two and a half hours on the surface of the moon, conducting a variety of experiments. They also collected samples of soil and rocks to bring back to Earth.

As a reminder, the astronauts left a raised American flag on the moon's surface to mark their amazing accomplishment!

The three astronauts returned to earth in the Command Module "Columbia" on July 24, 1969 having successfully completed its mission.

Read *First Man on the Moon* and answer questions

1. The first man on the moon was

◯ John F. Kennedy.   ◯ Neil Armstrong.   ◯ Edwin (Buzz) Aldrin.   ◯ Michael Collins.

2. Neil Armstrong stepped onto the moon on

◯ May 21, 1961.   ◯ July 16, 1969.   ◯ July 19, 1969.   ◯ July 20, 1969.

3. The astronauts could jump higher on the moon because

◯ they are stronger.   ◯ there is less gravity on the moon.

◯ there is more gravity on the moon.   ◯ there is no air to breathe.

4. The portable life support system

◯ controls the temperature inside the suit.

◯ controls the temperature and pressure inside the suit.

◯ provides oxygen and controls the temperature and pressure inside the suit.

◯ controls the atmosphere outside the suit.

5. The astronauts probably collected samples of soil and rocks and brought them back to Earth to

◯ see what they are made up of.   ◯ grow better plants.

◯ give to people as souvenirs.   ◯ put in museums.

6. This text is

◯ an information report.   ◯ a factual recount.   ◯ a narrative.   ◯ an explanation.

EVERY DROP COUNTS
Saving water starts in your own backyard

On average, people use a quarter of their household water on the garden.

This is placing a great strain on our rivers.

Buy by doing some simple things you can

reduce your water consumption and ensure

there will always be enough....

for us and the environment.

1. Only water when your garden needs it. Check soil first to see if it's dry.
2. Water early in the morning or the evening rather than in the middle of the day to reduce water lost through evaporation.
3. Mulching helps the soil retain water and reduces evaporation by up to 70%.
4. Plant local natives that use less water and use low maintenance.
5. Use a trigger nozzle on your hose.
6. Fit a time and rain switch to your watering system to prevent overwatering.
7. Water the base of plants, not the leaves or flowers, and do so slowly and deeply.
8. Cover your pool to reduce evaporation - this can save up to 30,000 litres per year.
9. Check your meter to detect any leaking pipes.
10. Install a rainwater tank.
    For more information visit www.livingthing.net.au

Read *Every Drop Counts* on page and answer questions

1. The main idea in the text is to

- ◯ encourage people to use less water.
- ◯ water your garden carefully.
- ◯ make sure we don't pollute the water.
- ◯ buy rainwater tanks.

2. We should "Water early in the morning or the evening…" because

- ◯ people are at work during the day.
- ◯ you pay less for water at these times.
- ◯ it is not as hot at these times so less water gets evaporated.
- ◯ plants need water early in the morning.

3. You should check your water meter regularly because

- ◯ sometimes it breaks down.
- ◯ the water company doesn't check the meters.
- ◯ people may steal it.
- ◯ some pipes might leak which means you waste more water.

4. The title of the poster "Every Drop Counts" means

- ◯ we should count each drop of water.
- ◯ we should monitor our use of water.
- ◯ save more water in your backyard.
- ◯ plant less trees so we don't have to water as much

5. "This is placing a strain on our rivers" means

- ◯ our rivers are too full.
- ◯ water gets wasted and ends up in our rivers.
- ◯ we allow rain to flow into our rivers.
- ◯ we should ban pools from backyards.

6. "Saving water starts in your own backyard." means

- ◯ save more water in your backyard.
- ◯ governments need to be more responsible when saving water.
- ◯ people should not grow plants and trees in backyards.
- ◯ each person must take responsibility for saving water.

MAROONED ON AN ISLAND

You are going to write a story or narrative.

The idea for your story is "Marooned on an Island".

Where is the island? How did you get there?

How many people are with you? What dangers might there be?

What is on the island? How are you going to be saved?

Think about:

- the characters and where they are
- the problem or complication to be solved
- how the story will end

Remember to

- plan your story before you begin
- write in sentences
- choose your words carefully, watch spelling and punctuation
- use paragraphs
- edit and check your writing when you have finished

PRACTICE 2 ○ ○ ○

The spelling mistake in each sentence has been circled. In the box next to each question, write the correct spelling for each circled word.

1. Do you know the (anser) to the question?

2. "I never (ment) to hurt you," cried the boy.

3. We had a (truely) wonderful day at the beach.

4. Because Sam fainted we took him (strait) to the hospital.

5. The (docter) ordered Sam to undergo a series of tests.

6. "I will bring your main meal in just a (minit") said the waiter.

7. At the party there was (enuff) food to feed an army.

8. The millionaire owns a (bizniss) in Double Bay.

The spelling mistakes in these labels have been circled. In the box next to each question, write the correct spelling for each circled word.

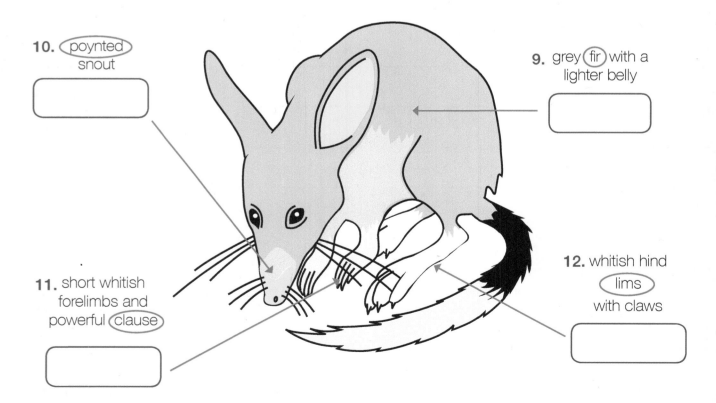

10. (poynted) snout

9. grey (fir) with a lighter belly

11. short whitish forelimbs and powerful (clause)

12. whitish hind (lims) with claws

Each of these sentences has one word that is incorrect. In the box next to each question, write the correct spelling for each circled word.

13. "My birthday is in (Febuery,) stated Christian.

14. (Insted) of hamburgers we are buying pizza this evening.

15. Mr Davis is a (teecher) who likes to use technology.

16. The class can work quietly by (themselfs.)

Each of these sentences has one word that is incorrect. In the box next to each question, write the correct spelling for each circled word.

17. Carlo decorated the (Crissmas) tree.

18. We had to (restrane) our dog from attacking the cat.

19. The Police brought the criminal to (justis.)

20. If the car had not (stopt) the little girl would have been hurt.

21. Do you have any (objecsion) to me borrowing your ladder?

22. Our friend, Brenden has the manners of a (gentelmen.)

23. Our water (suply) was cut because the pipes burst.

24. Collecting stamps gives me a great deal of (plesure.)

25. "In which (direkshion) is the shopping centre?" asked Gran.

Read the text *The Bushwalk*. Choose the correct words that fill the gaps in the text.

Shade one bubble.

26. He headed off into the bush, taking great care not to scratch _____ arms and legs on the thorny bushes.

   ○ he
   ○ his
   ○ she
   ○ her

27. He knew that the wild dingos in the bush would not hurt _____.

   ○ she
   ○ her
   ○ it
   ○ him

28. _____ looked around to make sure that he was not being followed.

   ○ Carefully, she
   ○ carefully, he
   ○ Carefully, he
   ○ Carefully, his

Shade one bubble.

29. Which sentence contains the correct punctuation?

   ○ What a fantastic catch!   ○ What is your name!
   ○ What fun we shall have at the theme park?   ○ What are we going to do!

30. Which sentence contains the correct punctuation?

   ○ "Have you seen my car keys." asked Dad.
   ○ "Have you seen my car keys? asked Dad.
   ○ "Have you seen my car keys," asked Dad.
   ○ "Have you seen my car keys?" asked Dad.

31. Which word makes this sentence make sense?

   _____ I was washing the dishes, Dad was drying them.

   ○ During   ○ While   ○ Before   ○ Even

PRACTICE 2

Shade two bubbles.

32. Where should the missing speech marks (" ") go?

○　　　　　　○　　　　○　　　　　　　　　　○

I think I saw a ghost! cried Natalie as she jumped up from her seat.

Shade one bubble.

33. Which word correctly completes the sentence?

The boy was _____ after a seagull stole his chips.

cries　　　　　cried　　　　　crying　　　　　cry

○　　　　　○　　　　　○　　　　　○

34. Which word correctly completes the sentence?

A box of jewels was _____ by the pirates.

hide　　　　　hidden　　　　　hiding　　　　　hides

○　　　　　○　　　　　○　　　　　○

Read the text *Mars – The Red Planet*. Choose the correct word to fit in each gap.

Shade one bubble.

Mars – The Red Planet

Mars is the fourth planet _____35._____ the Sun and the seventh

largest of the planets _____36._____ the Solar System. It probably

got its name because of its red colour. This planet is sometimes

_____37._____ as the "Red Planet". _____38._____ Mars has some

interesting features such as Olympus Mons, _____39._____

is the largest mountain in the Solar System rising to 24 000 metres high.

Hellas Planitia is a huge crater in the southern hemisphere on Mars. It is over 6 000 metres deep!

35. ○ at　　　　○ in　　　　○ from　　　　○ on

36. ○ in　　　　○ near　　　　○ at　　　　○ from

37. ○ name　　　　○ seen　　　　○ called　　　　○ known

38. ○ Besides Earth,　　○ But Earth,　　○ While Earth,　　○ Now Earth,

39. ○ which　　　　○ that　　　　○ what　　　　○ and

Read the text *Roller Coaster*. Choose the correct word to fit in each gap.

Shade one bubble.

Roller Coaster

40. As the Doom Rider slowly climbed the hill,

Nat and Lily held _____ to the

roll bar.

- ◯ tight
- ◯ tightly
- ◯ tightest
- ◯ tights

41. It reached the top, turned, then zoomed down

the steep slope. The girls screamed as the

Doom Rider twisted, turned and looped the

loop. _____ gasped when the

Doom Rider suddenly dropped, causing

them to feel a little ill.

- ◯ She
- ◯ I
- ◯ We
- ◯ They

42. Which word makes this sentence correct?

Bianca _____ go to the movies last Sunday.

can't	couldn't	won't	would
◯	◯	◯	◯

43. Which word makes this sentence correct?

_____ of these bags are yours?

Whose	What	Who's	Which
◯	◯	◯	◯

44. Which word or words makes this sentence correct?

At the fancy dress party, Jade wore a silly costume but Angela's was _____
of them all.

sillier	the sillier	the silliest	silly
◯	◯	◯	◯

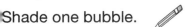
Shade one bubble.

45. Which word describes the house?

Mohammed, a fireman, walked (quickly) down the (quiet) corridor and into the (burning) house.

46. Which of these sentences should end in a question mark?

○ When the sun comes up I will go shopping

○ When the bus arrives I will pay for my ticket

○ When will you travel to the city

○ When you finish your dinner you may go outside

47. Which option completes the sentence correctly.

Kelly bought _____ to prepare for school.

○ books, pens and pencils   ○ books pens, and pencils

○ books, pens, and, pencils   ○ books pens and pencils

48. Which word or words makes this sentence correct?

The boys were dirty because they _____.

○ are playing in the mud   ○ had been playing in the mud

○ would be playing in the mud   ○ has been playing in the mud

49. Where should you place the missing comma?

Although ⬆ he was injured ⬆ Tom still played soccer ⬆ and softball ⬆ each week.

○   ○   ○   ○

50. Which sentence uses the apostrophe (') correctly?

○ We had seen Trinh's books in the library.

○ We had seen Trinhs' books in the library.

○ We had seen Trinhs book's in the library.

○ We had seen Trinhs books' in the library.

PRACTICE 2 ○ ○ ○

Australian Lizards

BOYD'S FOREST DRAGON: A forest dragon that is found in Queensland from Townsville to Cairns. It has large pointed scales on a crest behind its head. It spends most of its time in trees and keeps itself well camouflaged. They eat ants, crickets, spiders and beetles.

Size: About 15 centimetres but its tail adds more to its overall length.

FRILLED-NECK LIZARD: These lizards spend most of their lives in trees (arboreal). They can be found in the northern parts of Australia and also in New Guinea. Frilled-neck lizards have large, thin frills around their heads, which they display to frighten enemies. To further scare enemies, it opens its mouth wide and runs quickly on its hind legs. These lizards are carnivorous. They eat small lizards and bugs such as ants and cicadas

Size: Adult lizards are over 20 centimetres long.

GOANNA: The Goanna is found widely throughout Australia. It has a long flat body, strong limbs, sharp claws and a tail, which it uses to strike at enemies. They usually dig their own burrow systems for shelter. The Goanna eats insects, scorpions, spiders, centipedes and sometimes-small mammals. They will also dig out the eggs of lizards and turtles.

Size: Head to body length is 65 centimetres but their overall length can be up to 160 centimetres.

EASTERN BLUE-TONGUED LIZARD: These lizards can be found in a wide variety forests, grasslands, woodlands as well as in suburban backyards along the east coast of Australia. They are silver in colour with dark brown bands. They use their blue tongues to scare off enemies. They feed on a diet of slugs, snails, insects, wildflowers and berries.

Size: Eastern Blue-tongued Lizards can grow to 50 centimetres in length.

Read *Australian Lizards* on page and answer questions

1. The lizard with powerful limbs is the

○ Boyd's Forest Dragon. ○ Frilled-Neck Lizard. ○ Eastern Blue-tongued lizard. ○ Goanna.

2. The arboreal lizards are

○ Eastern Blue-tongued Lizard and the Frilled-Neck Lizard.

○ Goanna and Boyd's Forest Dragon.

○ Eastern Blue-tongued Lizard and the Goanna.

○ Boyd's Forest Dragon and the Frilled-Neck Lizard.

3. This text is about lizards that

○ may be found in suburbs and towns of Australia. ○ are native to Australia.

○ are carnivores. ○ live in trees.

4. The lizards in this text all

○ protect themselves in some way. ○ live in different countries.

○ are the same length. ○ have long tails.

5. The main purpose of the text is to

○ tell the reader what lizards eat. ○ explain how lizards protect themselves.

○ give information about some Australian lizards. ○ explain how to care for Australian lizards.

6. Information from this text would most probably be used by

○ scientists. ○ school students. ○ pet owners. ○ biologists.

The Jungle by Rob Stanley

Tom dreamed about living in the jungle amongst the wild animals but he was really in his backyard at home.

Tom flung himself out of the back door and landed on the soft grass. In his mind the grass was long, thick and bushy. He peered through the grass searching for the lion. In the treetops the monkeys screeched and chattered overhead as if they were laughing at him. He ignored their teasing and moved on.

The warm wind blew gently, rustling the grass. Suddenly a zebra startled Tom by bounding out of the bushes. It stood majestically in front of Tom with unblinking eyes. Its black and white coat dazzled Tom. The zebra sniffed the air, twitched its nose and raced off.

Tom got his binoculars out and searched the jungle for the lion. Through the lens he could see a pair of brightly coloured toucans sitting outside their hole in the tree. Their croaks frightened him but still he moved on.

Tom turned quickly when he heard the roar. He moved towards the sound, crouching low so as not to be spotted.

Just then, there was a cry.

'Tom! Dinner's ready!"

He would find the lion another day.

Read *The Jungle* and answer questions

1. What was Tom searching for?

○ a lion.　　　○ a zebra.　　　○ animals.　　　○ monkeys.

2. Which word tells us that the monkeys were above Tom?

○ jungle.　　　○ overhead.　　　○ bounding.　　　○ low.

3. "The Jungle" is a story about

○ a fearless hunter named Tom.　　　○ a boy's imagination.

○ animals in the jungle.　　　○ hunting for lions.

4. Tom ignored the teasing of the monkeys because

○ he was in a hurry to find the lion.　　　○ they annoyed him.

○ he didn't want to hurt them.　　　○ he was hungry.

5. Tom stopped searching for the lion because

○ he was tired.　　　○ he was being teased by the monkeys.

○ It was hard to find.　　　○ it was time for dinner.

6. Write the numbers 1 to 4 in the boxes to show the events of the story in order.

☐ A pair of toucans frightened Tom.　　　☐ The monkeys teased Tom.

☐ Tom ran out the back door.　　　☐ Tom went inside the house to have dinner.

Some students surveyed their classmates on which season they liked the best. They gathered their information and wrote reasons why one season was better than the other.

Which is Better?
Summer or Winter?

Many people love to spend long summer days
doing enjoyable activities.
Summer is better than winter.

To begin with, summer means extra hours of daylight through Daylight Savings. Putting the clock forward an hour means that you can spend more of your time outside. You can go to the beach, swim in the ocean and sunbake in the shade. We can also participate in other exciting outdoor activities such as fishing, camping and sailing. When it is time to go home there will be enough daylight to go out and play with friends.

As well, summer is much more pleasant. You can usually wear tee shirts, shorts and thongs instead of rugging up in the winter cold wearing heavy jackets, jumpers and jeans. This also means that you have less washing to do, which saves water. Clothes can then be hung outside to dry, which saves electricity from the clothes drier.

Another reason is that most of the school holidays occur in summer. We usually have about six weeks of holidays. This allows us to go overseas or to other states to enjoy the fine weather, see new places and meet new people. There is nothing nicer than eating an ice cream on a hot day. In winter we usually have to stay indoors because it is cold, windy and raining. It is boring sitting in your house with nothing to do.

To conclude, summer is better than winter because the weather is comfortable, there are more activities to keep children occupied and people spend more time with friends because there are more hours of daylight.

Read *Which is Better? Summer or Winter?* and answer the questions.

1. What was the focus of the students' survey?

◯ to explain why it's fun to go to the beach.   ◯ to give reasons why winter is not a good season

◯ to find out which season was better.   ◯ to give reasons why summer is a good season.

2. Why did the author write a question as the title of the text?

◯ to get readers to think carefully about the topic.   ◯ to make the readers angry.

◯ to argue that you can do fun things in summer.   ◯ because the author is an expert.

3. In summer, we can save on electricity bills by

◯ washing our clothes.   ◯ hanging our clothes outside on the clothes line.

◯ putting our washing in the clothes drier.   ◯ ironing our clothes.

4. The purpose of the text is to

◯ get people to hang their clothes outside.   ◯ encourage people to go out in summer.

◯ wear heavy jackets in winter.   ◯ convince people that summer is the better season.

5. "As well, summer is much more pleasant." This paragraph is mainly about

◯ being environmentally friendly.   ◯ buying clothes for winter.

◯ school holidays.   ◯ pleasant summer weather.

6. There are more hours of daylight because

◯ there are 25 hours a day in summer.   ◯ the clocks are put forward an hour.

◯ you can play with your friends.   ◯ the clocks are put back an hour.

ATTACK OF THE TARANTULAS

You are going to write a story or narrative.

The idea for your story is "Attack of the Tarantulas".

Where and when did this happen? Describe the tarantulas.

Who is with you? What might happen?

What can the tarantulas do??

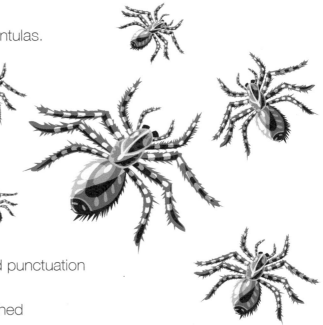

Think about:

- the characters and where they are
- the problem or complication to be solved
- how the story will end

Remember to

- plan your story before you begin
- write in sentences
- choose your words carefully, watch spelling and punctuation
- use paragraphs
- edit and check your writing when you have finished

_____

_____

_____

_____

_____

_____

_____

_____

_____

_____

_____

_____

The spelling mistake in each sentence has been circled. In the box next to each question, write the correct spelling for each circled word.

1. Lisa got into (trubble) because she threw a pencil across the room.

2. The two (womin) had their handbags stolen.

3. On (wensday) we will be going on an excursion to the farm.

4. Maria needs to improve her (gramer) when writing.

5. We (offen) go shopping for groceries at Woolies.

6. "Would you like a (peece) of cake?" asked Mum.

7. We (cood) see the spectacular fireworks display from the balcony.

8. It was hard to speak because his throat was (horse.)

The spelling mistakes in these labels have been circled. In the box next to each question, write the correct spelling for each circled word.

The Water Cycle

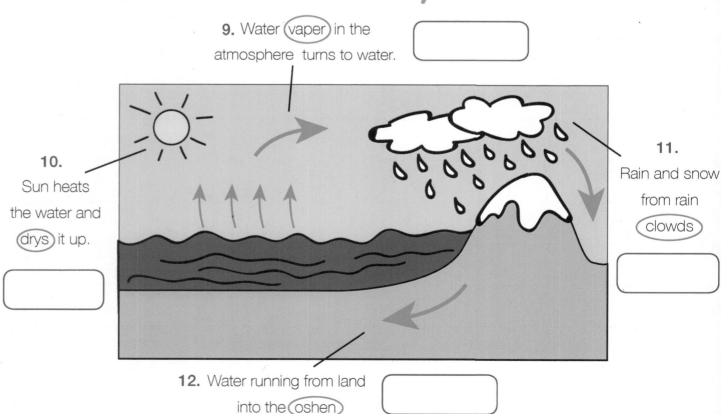

9. Water (vaper) in the atmosphere turns to water.

10. Sun heats the water and (drys) it up.

11. Rain and snow from rain (clowds)

12. Water running from land into the (oshen)

Each of these sentences has one word that is incorrect. In the box next to each question, write the correct spelling for each circled word.

13. "Can you (gess) what's in the box?" asked Hameed.

14. Josh continued playing even (thoe) he had hurt his knee.

15. My helper will (asist) me with this magic trick.

16. All of a (suddan) there was a crack of thunder.

Each of these sentences has one word that is incorrect. In the box next to each question, write the correct spelling for each circled word.

17. Mum will help me to (orgenise) Dad's birthday party.

18. We look (forwerd) to Grandpa visiting us from Adelaide.

19. The Counsellor asked me to discuss a (personel) matter.

20. The teacher had to (promt) Shaun to get him to speak.

21. The Principal was going to (summen) the bully to the office.

22. Our neighbours will be going on (vaycaytion).

23. The witness to the accident was asked to make a (statment).

24. My doctor is going to (refur) me to a surgeon for an operation.

25. We discussed a matter of great (importence).

Read the text *The Haunted House..* Choose the correct words that fill the gaps in the text.

Shade one bubble. 🖉

The Haunted House

26. They crept carefully into the house hoping that nothing would scare _____.

- ○ him
- ○ us
- ○ they
- ○ them

27. A skeleton suddenly appeared and the girls screamed. The skeleton was chasing _____.

- ○ us
- ○ them
- ○ you
- ○ both

28. _____ raced out of the house and never went back there again.

- ○ Swiftly, we
- ○ Swiftly, they
- ○ Swiftly, she
- ○ Swiftly, I

Shade one bubble. 🖉

29. Which sentence contains the correct punctuation?

- ○ How wonderful your picture is!
- ○ How beautiful those flowers are?
- ○ How are you feeling today!
- ○ How hungry are you!

30. Which sentence contains the correct punctuation?

- ○ "Will you be attending the excursion?" asked the teacher.
- ○ "Will you be attending the excursion? asked the teacher.
- ○ "will you be attending the excursion?" asked the teacher.
- ○ "Will you be attending the excursion," asked the teacher.

31. Which word makes this sentence make sense?

_____ the movie, Dad was munching on popcorn.

- ○ During
- ○ While
- ○ Because
- ○ Even

Shade two bubbles.

32. Where should the missing speech marks (" and ") go?

In front of the jury, the defendant cried, I did not rob the jewellery store.

Shade one bubble.

33. Which word correctly completes the sentence?

Emad went skating on the pond because it was _____.

freezing   freezes   froze   frozen

34. Which word correctly completes the sentence?

Grace _____ a good cartwheel on the mat yesterday.

done   does   did   do

Read the text *Frill-Necked Lizard*. Choose the correct word to fit in each gap.

Shade one bubble.

Frill-Necked Lizard

The frill-necked lizard is found only in northern Australia and southern New Guinea. It is given

_____35._____ name because of the large frill around _____36._____ neck which usually stays folded

close to the body.

The frill-necked lizard spends most of its time in trees and it _____37._____

mainly on insects and small vertebrates.

An interesting fact is that _____38._____ creatures have a range of colours

from orange and red _____39._____ brown and grey.

35. ◯ these   ◯ those   ◯ a   ◯ this

36. ◯ its   ◯ it's   ◯ his   ◯ her

37. ◯ eats   ◯ feeds   ◯ fed   ◯ ate

38. ◯ them   ◯ these   ◯ those   ◯ that

39. ◯ to   ◯ and   ◯ from   ◯ then

Read the text *Runaway Car*. Choose the correct word to fit in each gap.

Shade one bubble.

Runaway Car

40. The car rolled _____ down
    the hill towards the cliff. The hand
    brake had not been applied.

    ○ slowly
    ○ slowest
    ○ slow
    ○ slows

41. A group of girls crossed the
    road at the end of the street.
    _____ screamed
    as the car hurtled past out of
    harm's way

    ○ She
    ○ I
    ○ We
    ○ They

42. Which word makes this sentence correct?

    Once mum has _____ the eggs she can make the cake.

    beat   beaten   beats   beated
    ○   ○   ○   ○

43. Which word makes this sentence correct?

    To _____ was the letter addressed?

    who   whose   whom   which
    ○   ○   ○   ○

44. Which word or words makes this sentence correct?

    At Antonio's party, Charlie told a funny joke but Crystal's was _____ of them all.

    the funniest   the funnier   funny   fun
    ○   ○   ○   ○

Shade one bubble.

45. Which word describes how Frank put up the sail on his boat?

Despite the (ferocious) winds, Frank (calmly) hoisted the sail and (quickly) sailed back to shore.

46. Which of these sentences should end in an exclamation mark?

- ◯ What a beautiful bunch of flowers
- ◯ What shall I do with the food that is left over
- ◯ What are you doing with my pen
- ◯ What can you do with this gadget

47. Which option completes the sentence correctly.

Brittany brought _____ to school.

- ◯ A tuna sandwich, an apple, and a drink.
- ◯ A tuna sandwich an apple, and a drink.
- ◯ a tuna sandwich, an apple, and a drink.
- ◯ a tuna sandwich, an apple and a drink.

48. Which word or words makes this sentence correct?

Dianne was recovering at home because she _____.

- ◯ is in hospital
- ◯ had been in hospital
- ◯ would be in hospital
- ◯ might be in hospital

49. Where should you place the missing comma?

Because ▲ food costs are rising daily ▲ many people ▲ are now buying ▲ cheaper groceries.

◯ ◯ ◯ ◯

50. Which sentence uses the apostrophe (') correctly?

- ◯ Harrys crayons' had been taken from his bag.
- ◯ Harrys' crayons had been taken from his bag.
- ◯ Harrys crayon's had been taken from his bag.
- ◯ Harry's crayons had been taken from his bag.

PRACTICE 3 ○○○

Sammy Spy – Kid Detective by Rob Stanley

A number of lunches had recently gone missing in Class 5S. This time Mr Stewart's lunch had mysteriously disappeared from the lunch basket. Sammy Spy had taken on the case.

"Who were the lunch monitors today?" asked Sammy Spy."

Sammy rubbed his tousled, yellow hair and screwed up his face. He was a short, Year 5 student but quite an intelligent one. He loved nothing more than watching the crime channel on television and dreaming of the day when he could become a famous detective. In the meantime, this freckle-faced student had devoted all his energy to solving the case of the missing lunches. He stared at the lunch basket but could see no sign of Mr Stewart's egg and lettuce sandwich.

"The monitors were Sarah Callen and Freddy Manning," replied Van Nguyen, another student in the class.

Sammy's eagle eyes spotted something yellow on the floor.

"Hmmm, what have we here?" he asked.

Sammy picked up the evidence and placed it in a plastic bag before Jack, his faithful basset hound could swallow it.

Sammy's eyes scanned each student sitting in the classroom, searching for expressions of guilt. Was it quiet Jane Masters, the girl who was so well behaved in class? Or Bruiser McGhee the class bully who smirked at him as if he knew whom the criminal was?

"I will identify the criminal very easily," announced Sammy Spy. "I want you all to stand up.

"Mr Stewart, as I walk past each student would you ask each one to open his or her mouth?" he asked.

Read Sammy Spy - Kid Detective and answer the questions.

1. This text is

○ a procedure.   ○ an information report.   ○ a recount.   ○ a narrative.

2. Sarah and Freddy were probably suspects because

○ they were in Class 5S.   ○ they were the lunch monitors that day.

○ they both liked food.   ○ they were both hungry.

3. "Sammy's eagle eyes" means

○ that his eyesight is very good.   ○ Sammy had seen an eagle.

○ Sammy followed the eagles.   ○ Sammy used to have an eagle for a pet.

4. ..something yellow on the floor was probably

○ some of his yellow hair.   ○ butter from the sandwich.

○ a piece of pineapple.   ○ a small piece of egg.

5. Sammy Spy asked each student to open his or her mouth because

○ he wanted to see if there was any food.

○ he wanted to see how big each mouth was.

○ he wanted to look down their throats.

○ he wanted to smell their breath.

6. Jack was

○ an eagle.   ○ a dog.   ○ a cat.   ○ a student.

How to Make a Cork Boat

It is very simple to make a boat from cork. The children will have hours of fun sailing them in puddles, baths and streams.

Equipment
- corks
- matchsticks or cocktail sticks
- a small knife (to be used by an adult)
- large leaves from the garden or a piece of paper
- a pair of scissors

Procedure
1. Cut a cork in two equal halves.
2. Cut the cocktail sticks in half.
3. Place each half of the cocktail stick into the side of one of the pieces of cork.
4. Push the cork with the cocktail sticks into the other piece of cork.
5. Push one piece of cocktail stick into the flat side of the cork to act as a mast.
6. Push leaves through the cocktail sticks to make sails.
7. Find somewhere to sail your cork boat.
8. Experiment with different designs.

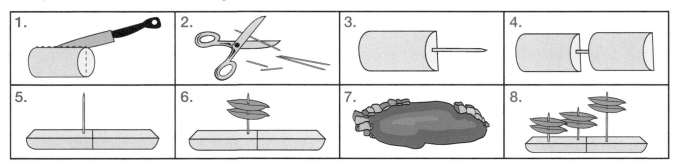

Read *How to Make a Cork Boat* and answer the questions.

1. This text is
- ○ a procedure.
- ○ an information report.
- ○ a recount.
- ○ a narrative.

2. A small knife is probably used to
- ○ cut leaves.
- ○ cut the cork.
- ○ make holes in the cork.
- ○ cut the boat in half.

3. You can use the cocktail stick
- ○ as a mast.
- ○ to make oars.
- ○ as a boat.
- ○ to sail on the water.

4. The cocktail sticks are probably
- ○ broken in half with your hands.
- ○ used as sails.
- ○ sliced carefully into small pieces.
- ○ cut in half with a pair of scissors.

5. The main purpose of the text is to
- ○ use different types of equipment.
- ○ help children who are bored.
- ○ show how to make something using cheap materials.
- ○ show people how to make a simple boat out of cork.

6. The best place to sail the cork boats would be
- ○ a river.
- ○ the bath tub.
- ○ the beach.
- ○ in a storm.

7. Experiment with different designs probably means
- ○ use different materials.
- ○ make a different type of transport.
- ○ make different types of boats with the materials.
- ○ make a boat out of wood.

PRACTICE 3 ○○○

The Glow by Rob Stanley

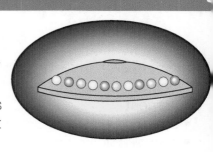

The West family had just gone to bed but Simon West; an eleven-year-old boy could sense that this particular night was going to be very different.

Simon tossed and turned in his sleep. The only time he had felt this jumpy was each Christmas Eve when he was dying to guess what Santa would bring. But this was not Christmas Eve.

Just as he had reached the moment when he was neither asleep nor awake, a surge of heat went through his body. Simon opened his eyes to a hazy glow filling the room. It was coming from outside.

He tiptoed to the curtains and drew it slightly to one side. What he saw in his front yard astounded him. A large silver disc like a big saucepan lid was glowing and humming. Red, yellow and silver lights revolved around its middle as if advertising a circus or a theme park.

Simon looked out over the town. Amazingly, no one else had stirred. It was as if everyone else had been frozen in time.

Suddenly there was a long whirring noise and a thin silver walkway began to stretch out from the disc. Simon's heart pounded like a drum and his mouth went dry. He gasped in amazement as a little creature waddled along the walkway. Like the silver disc, its wide head looked like a saucepan lid but its face was grey. It had two wide almond-shaped eyes, two holes for a nose and thin matchstick lips. A triangular body, covered by a silver suit was attached to the head by a long, thin, bony neck. It waddled out on short, stubby three-toed feet. Simon stood open-mouthed, unable to speak. He could hardly believe what he was seeing! The creature raised its two, stubby glowing arms towards Simon. Its thin lips did not move but somehow it spoke. "Mama!" it cried.

Read The Glow on page and answer questions

1. The silver disc was probably

⬭ an alien.　　⬭ a space ship.　　⬭ a car.　　⬭ a plane.

2. Which word tells us that Simon became hot very quickly?

⬭ surge　　⬭ hazy　　⬭ glow　　⬭ lights

3. Simon was having trouble sleeping because

⬭ it was Christmas Eve.　　⬭ he was hot.

⬭ he wanted to stay awake to see Santa.

⬭ he could sense that something was going to happen.

4. Simon awoke because

⬭ he suddenly felt hot.　　⬭ a hazy glow filled the room.

⬭ he heard Santa.　　⬭ there was a long whirring noise.

5. The long whirring noise was caused by

⬭ the hazy glow.　　⬭ the creature's head.

⬭ the silver walkway.　　⬭ Simon's heart.

6. Write the numbers 1 to 4 in the boxes to show the events of the story in order.

☐ Simon's heart was beating hard.　　☐ A hazy glow filled the room.

☐ A silver disc landed in Simon's front yard.　　☐ A creature waddled out of the disc.

THE INTERNET IS A GOOD THING

What do you think of this statement? Write a text to convince the audience of your opinions.

Think about:

- whether you agree, disagree or see both sides of the argument
- an introduction – introduce ideas by clearly saying what you think about the topic
- your arguments – give reasons or evidence to explain
- a conclusion – give a summary of the main points of your argument

Remember to

- plan your writing
- write in good sentences
- pay attention to spelling and punctuation
- choose words carefully to convince the audience of your opinions
- use a new paragraph when writing about a new idea
- edit your writing so that it makes sense

The spelling mistake in each sentence has been circled. In the box next to each question, write the correct spelling for each circled word.

1. This is the house (wear) I grew up.

2. Our school is trying to (raze) money for charity.

3. Mum stayed home from work because she had a bad (coff.)

4. After the marathon Robert's legs began to (ake.)

5. The rundown old house was (bilt) in 1877.

6. "I do not (belive) in ghosts," stated Mum.

7. We (cood) see the spectacular fireworks display from the balcony.

8. It was a wonderful day to walk (amung) the flowers in the garden.

The spelling mistakes in these labels have been circled. In the box next to each question, write the correct spelling for each circled word.

Farm to Table

9. Seeds are (plantered.)

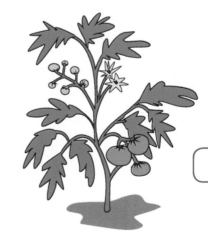

10. The plants (gro) and become ripe for picking.

11. The produce is picked and put into a (barskit.)

12. Fruit and (vegtabuls) are delivered to the stores by truck.

Each of these sentences has one word that is incorrect.
In the box next to each question, write the correct spelling
for each circled word.

13.   "Would you like some (shooger) in your coffee?" asked Dad.

14.   Grandpa's pants fell down because they were (lose.)

15.   The judge will (imprisen) him for robbing the bank.

16.   Please reply to my letter at your (erlyest) convenience.

Each of these sentences has one word that is incorrect. In the box next to each question, write the correct spelling for each circled word.

17. Mum organised a clown to (entertane) us at the party.

18. Marney had (diffcultie) with spelling.

19. Chris and Alan are going to the stadium to (serport) their team.

20. The job at the museum pays a good (salery.)

21. The detective drove quickly to the (seen) of the crime.

22. Samuel Barsby was the first (convick) to be flogged in NSW.

23. A ferocious storm could easily (reck) the little boat.

24. (Finerlly,) we arrived at the Gold Coast after a long drive.

25. Our class will (debait) the issue of which pets are best.

PRACTICE 4 ○○○

Read the text *The Bermuda Triangle*. Choose the correct words that fill the gaps in the text.

Shade one bubble.

The Bermuda Triangle

26. The Bermuda Triangle is a region in the western part of the North Atlantic Ocean in which a number of aircraft and ships _____ disappeared mysteriously.

- ○ has
- ○ have
- ○ are
- ○ were

27. A US navy ship called the USS Cyclops disappeared in _____ area in 1918. A crew of 309 people went missing without a trace.

- ○ those
- ○ this
- ○ them
- ○ then

28. _____ were never seen again.

- ○ Unfortunately, we
- ○ Unfortunately, they
- ○ Unfortunately, you
- ○ Unfortunately, I

Shade one bubble.

29. Which sentence contains the correct punctuation?

- ○ My name is Albert John Farmer.
- ○ What glorious weather we are having.
- ○ Can you touch your elbow with your tongue!
- ○ Get out of my way?

30. Which sentence contains the correct punctuation?

- ○ "John Oxley was a famous Australian explorer?" stated the teacher.
- ○ John Oxley was a famous Australian explorer, "stated the teacher."
- ○ "John Oxley was a famous australian explorer?" stated the teacher.
- ○ "John Oxley was a famous Australian explorer," stated the teacher.

31. Which word makes this sentence make sense?

_____ to the wet weather, the tennis match has been delayed.

- ○ Down
- ○ Because
- ○ Due
- ○ Despite

PRACTICE 4

Shade two bubbles.

32. Where should the missing speech marks (" and ") go?

As ⃝ Ned Kelly was about to be hanged, ⃝ he cried, ⃝ Such is life! ⃝

Shade one bubble.

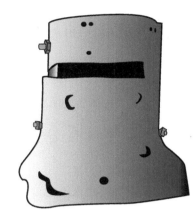

33. Which word correctly completes the sentence?

When Daniel _____ his can of soft drink it fizzed up.

shakes   shook   shaken   shaked
  ⃝   ⃝   ⃝   ⃝

34. Which word correctly completes the sentence?

Connor _____ to eat vegetables with every meal.

liken   liking   like   likes
  ⃝   ⃝   ⃝   ⃝

Read the text *Green Ringtail Possum*. Choose the correct word to fit in each gap.

Shade one bubble.

Green Ringtail Possum

The Green Ringtail Possum _____**35.**_____ greenish, soft, thick fur. This is _____**36.**_____ it has a

mixture of grey, black, yellow and white hairs. It has two silvery stripes along its vertebra with white

patches under its ears and eyes.

It is arboreal, which means that _____**37.**_____ spends most of its time in trees where it

_____**38.**_____ on leaves from different trees.

It is mainly nocturnal. It _____**39.**_____ the branch with one or both hind feet and sits on its coiled tail

with its front paws curled into its body.

35. ⃝ is   ⃝ was   ⃝ has   ⃝ have

36. ⃝ though   ⃝ because   ⃝ who   ⃝ so

37. ⃝ it   ⃝ he   ⃝ they   ⃝ she

38. ⃝ eats   ⃝ feeds   ⃝ fed   ⃝ ate

39. ⃝ grip   ⃝ grips   ⃝ gripped   ⃝ gripping

PRACTICE 4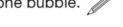

Read the text *How Does a Kite Fly?*. Choose the correct word to fit in each gap.

Shade one bubble. ✏️

How Does a Kite Fly?

40. A kite is an object which is usually made of a light material. The material is _____ over a frame. Because the material is light a kite will lift off from the ground and fly into the wind.

- ◯ stretch
- ◯ stretches
- ◯ stretched
- ◯ stretching

41. A kite uses the wind to make it fly because it is _____ than the air. The wind travels over the kite and is split into two streams of air. One of the streams goes above the kite while the second goes under the kite.

- ◯ heavy
- ◯ heavier
- ◯ heaviest
- ◯ heavily

42. Which word makes this sentence correct?

Marko _____ a new bag from the shop because the old one was tattered.

buy	bought	bring	brought
◯	◯	◯	◯

43. Which word makes this sentence correct?

Carol is the girl _____ father is in hospital?

whom	whose	who's	which
◯	◯	◯	◯

44. Which word or words makes this sentence correct?

When completing the Mathematics test most of the questions were easy but the addition question was the _____.

easy	easily	easier	easiest
◯	◯	◯	◯

Shade one bubble.

45. Which word describes how Lara felt about her dog?

Lara patted her dog (lovingly) as she (excitedly) told (news) reporters how he had saved her.

46. Which of these sentences is a statement?

◯ What a fantastic garden you have

◯ What I need is a hammer and nails

◯ What are you going to buy with your money

◯ What can you do with this gadget

47. Which option completes the sentence correctly.

May I have a _____ sandwich?

◯ cheese, tomato and, onion

◯ cheese tomato, and onion

◯ cheese, tomato, and onion

◯ cheese, tomato and onion

48. Which word or words makes this sentence correct?

Dad devoured the hamburger because he _____.

◯ is hungry   ◯ was hungry

◯ might be hungry   ◯ would be hungry

49. Where should you place the missing comma?

Recently Sandy went for a training session at the botanical gardens.

◯   ◯   ◯   ◯

50. Which sentence uses the apostrophe (') correctly?

◯ All of the students' projects were destroyed in the fire.

◯ All of the student's projects were destroyed in the fire.

◯ All of the students project's were destroyed in the fire.

◯ All of the students projects' were destroyed in the fire.

Hargraves Finds Gold

The great gold rush in California began early in 1848. Many people in Australia left their jobs, homes and farms to go to California to seek their fortune.

Edward Hargraves was one of these people who led a small group in 1850. He didn't find much but the terrain in California looked similar to a place he had been to in New South Wales. He returned home and headed west through the Blue Mountains.

On the Bathurst Plains he met a man named John Lister who had already found gold in the area. Lister took him to the place where he had found gold. Hargraves knew then that this area looked similar to California.

At Summerhill Creek, Hargraves panned for gold and managed to find a few specks. He then taught Lister and brothers William and James Tom the gold mining techniques he had learned in California.

The group excavated thirteen pounds worth of gold from Summerhill Creek. He returned to Sydney to inform the authorities of his find. On May 22, 1851 a gold discovery was announced and the gold rush was on!

Trips to California were cancelled and those who had been seeking their fortune in California now returned home. Indeed, many people from other countries also arrived on Australian shores in an effort to find wealth. Edward Hargraves was given ten thousand pounds and named Crown Commissioner of the Goldfields. He did not share his money with Lister or the Toms brothers and they became very upset. They took him to court but lost the case.

Because of the gold rushes, many new towns were built and transport links established. As well, migrants from overseas remained in Australia. Many were well educated and became involved in business, politics and other high profile jobs. This helped the nation to grow and prosper.

Read *Hargraves Finds Gold* and answer the questions.

1. The gold rush in Australia began in

   ◯ 1848.   ◯ 1851.   ◯ 1852.   ◯ 1850.

2. Hargraves headed west through the Blue Mountains because

   ◯ he couldn't find gold in California.   ◯ that was where he lived.

   ◯ he wanted to climb the Blue Mountains.   ◯ he knew the terrain there was similar to California.

3. William and James Tom learned how to find gold

   ◯ in California.   ◯ because John Lister taught them.

   ◯ because Edward Hargraves taught them.   ◯ in Sydney.

4. People probably stopped going to California because

   ◯ the gold ran out.   ◯ they couldn't afford to travel there.

   ◯ they could find gold in Australia.   ◯ Edward Hargraves told them to stay home.

5. The main purpose of the text is to

   ◯ recount how the first gold discoveries came to be known.

   ◯ explain that Hargraves was a thief.

   ◯ recount the first gold discoveries in Australia and how the country grew.

   ◯ name the person who discovered gold in Australia.

6. The gold rushes caused

   ◯ many new towns and transport links to be developed.   ◯ many people to lose their jobs.

   ◯ people to fight.   ◯ the destruction of many small towns.

The Australian Flag

The Union Jack is made up of the flags of St George, St Andrew and St Patrick. This is also the British flag. This part of the flag represents parliamentary democracy, freedom of speech and rule of law.

This constellation of five stars is called the Southern Cross. It represents our place in the Southern Hemisphere.

The Commonwealth Star has seven points, which represents the six states, and the seventh point represents all Australian territories.

On January 1 1901 celebrated the creation of a new nation, the Commonwealth of Australia. On April 29 1901 the Commonwealth Government announced a competition to design an Australian flag.

A total of 32 823 entries was received by men, women and children all over Australia. On September 3 1901, Lady Hopetoun, the wife of the Governor General opened a display of the entries at the Royal Exhibition Building in Melbourne. Sir Edmund Barton, the Prime Minister of Australia, announced five winners who submitted similar designs. Each of the winners received prize money of forty pounds.

In 1996, the Governor General, Sir William Deane, proclaimed that September the 3rd would be called "Australian National Flag Day" to commemorate the day in 1901 when the flag was first flown.

All Australians have the right and the privilege of flying the Australian National Flag.

Read *The Australian Flag* and answer the questions.

1. Australians began celebrating Australian National Flag Day in

◯ January 1901.　　◯ April 1901.　　◯ September 1901.　　◯ 1996.

2. The Union Jack is made up of

◯ the flags of St George, St Andrew and St Peter.

◯ the flags of St George, St Andrew and St Patrick.

◯ the constellation of five stars known as the Southern Cross.

◯ the Commonwealth Star representing six states and all territories.

3. The competition to design an Australian flag was won by

◯ five people.　　◯ Lady Hopetoun.　　◯ Sir Edmund Barton.　　◯ Sir William Deane.

4. The Southern Cross is part of the Australian flag because

◯ we have another flag called the Southern Cross.　　◯ it was used in the times of the gold rushes.

◯ it represents all states and territories.　　◯ it shows our place in the world.

5. The main purpose of the text is to

◯ explain how the Australian flag was designed and what it means.

◯ explain why we should celebrate Australian National Flag Day.

◯ recount the day that the five people won the flag competition.

◯ explain the meaning of the Union Jack.

6. The author probably wrote the text because

◯ he is a proud Australian.

◯ he wants people to know that they have the right to fly the flag.

◯ many people don't know the meaning behind the Australian flag.

◯ he wants people to remember the day Australia became a new nation.

PRACTICE 4 ○○○

Our Camp at Milson Island

Last Tuesday, sixty-five students and four teachers travelled to Milson Island Sport and Recreation camp for three days. We were going on camp to have some new outdoor recreational experiences.

We were all very excited when we arrived at school. We boarded the bus and left at 6.30 a.m. Most of us chatted excitedly about our trip but Carly fell asleep on the bus.

We had been on the bus for about two hours. We then had to catch a ferry, which would take us to Milson Island. We took our bags off the bus and some people on the ferry helped us aboard.

It was a beautiful, calm, sunny day and the ferry motored gently to Milson Island.

Some people who worked at the camp greeted us at the jetty. We collected our bags and walked up the hill to the camp. Now I wished I hadn't packed so many things in my bag!

When we arrived, the camp organiser spoke to us about the rules we were to follow at camp.

Next, we had something to eat and drink for recess. I had orange cordial and a juicy, red apple.

It was now time to go to our cabins. I chose a cabin with my friends Thomas, David and Minh. We quickly put our bags inside and raced down the hill to go to our first activity.

Minh and I were put in the Kookaburras group and David and Thomas were in the Koalas group. The Kookaburras went down to the high ropes course. The course was high off the ground and I gulped and looked anxiously at Minh. After listening to the safety talk we put on our gear and got our harnesses ready. Minh and I climbed the ladder ready for our turn.

Slowly we climbed out onto the course. Minh told me not to look down. We worked really well together and heaved a sigh of relief when we finished the course. What an achievement!

We returned to the dining room for lunch, which consisted of hot dogs and salad. Minh and I ate hungrily and chatted to Thomas and David who had been orienteering that morning.

We couldn't wait for the next activity!   *By Christopher Smith Class 6T*

Read *Our Camp to Milson Island* and answer the questions.

1. The trip to Milson Island took

   ◯ one hour.   ◯ two hours.   ◯ more than two hours.   ◯ half an hour.

2. The students and teachers went on camp to

   ◯ experience new ways to have fun outside.   ◯ have a holiday.

   ◯ see what life was like on Milson Island.   ◯ sleep in cabins.

3. Christopher "gulped and looked anxiously at Minh" because

   ◯ he hadn't worn a harness before.   ◯ he gets seasick.

   ◯ he's never been away from home before.   ◯ he probably doesn't like heights.

4. Christopher wished he hadn't packed so many things in his bag because

   ◯ his bag was messy.   ◯ he had to walk up the hill carrying his heavy bag.

   ◯ he couldn't choose which clothes to wear.   ◯ Mum would have more washing to do.

5. The main purpose of the text is to

   ◯ explain how to do the high ropes course.   ◯ recount the trip to camp.

   ◯ give the procedure for following camp rules.   ◯ explain the rules of the camp.

6. At lunchtime the children ate

   ◯ hamburgers.   ◯ hot dogs.   ◯ apples.   ◯ orange cordial.

TODAY'S CHILDREN ARE COUCH POTATOES.

Do you agree?

What do you think of this statement? Write a text to convince the audience of your opinions. Think about:

- whether you agree, disagree or see both sides of the argument
- an introduction – introduce ideas by clearly saying what you think about the topic
- your arguments – give reasons or evidence to explain
- a conclusion – give a summary of the main points of your argument

Remember to

- plan your writing
- write in good sentences
- pay attention to spelling and punctuation
- choose words carefully to convince the audience of your opinions
- use a new paragraph when writing about a new idea
- edit your writing so that it makes sense

The spelling mistake in each sentence has been circled. In the box next to each question, write the correct spelling for each circled word.

1. At the (begining) of the assembly we sang the National Anthem.

2. I don't know (wether) to go to the movies or stay home.

3. Uncle Jim and his family brought (thair) dog to our house.

4. The sisters will be sleeping in (seprate) bedrooms.

5. (Sinse) we have returned from holidays we have been busy.

6. Mum is going to (wair) her new outfit to the wedding.

7. The chicken (layd) a number of eggs in the chicken coop.

8. If you don't look after your phone you could (loose) it.

The spelling mistakes in these labels have been circled. In the box next to each question, write the correct spelling for each circled word.

Recycling at Home

9.

Collect paper, plastics and

(glarss) for recycling

10.

Empty and (rince) containers

and put them in the

recycling bin.

11.

When your recycling

bin is full take

it outside to be

(emptyed)

12.

Make (shore) food

waste is placed in

the organics bin.

Each of these sentences has one word that is incorrect. In the box next to each question, write the correct spelling for each circled word.

13. Dad goes to the gym every (Toosday.)

14. The circus will be (comeing) to town in February.

15. I (prefur) to read comics rather than books.

16. The new (ishoo) of Woman's Day is on sale now.

Each of these sentences has one word that is incorrect. In the box next to each question, write the correct spelling for each circled word.

17. We will (publeesh) a new cookery book each year.

18. Mr Brian Speldon is the (direckter) of our company.

19. A real (astate) agent sells houses.

20. If you slip you could fall and badly (injer) yourself.

21. The car accident was a very (unforchunet) event.

22. The (primry) colours are red, yellow and blue.

23. In a debate you should (elabberate) on each argument.

24. Harry Kewell had a (contrackt) to play for Liverpool.

25. I try to (espress) myself clearly when I speak.

PRACTICE 5 ○○○

Read the text *Horse Riding*. Choose the correct words that fill the gaps in the text.

Shade one bubble.

Horse Riding

26. Tara had _____ the horse around the paddock before it bucked, reared and threw her off.

- ○ ride
- ○ riding
- ○ rode
- ○ ridden

27. She fell to the ground holding her arm. Tara _____ out in pain and looked around for help.

- ○ cry
- ○ cries
- ○ crying
- ○ cried

28. _____ there was a doctor nearby.

- ○ Luck
- ○ luckily
- ○ Luckily
- ○ luck

Shade one bubble.

29. Which sentence contains the correct punctuation?

- ○ Don't ever do that again!
- ○ Don't you care about my feelings!
- ○ Don't you like brussel sprouts.
- ○ Don't you have a blue coat.

30. Which sentence contains the correct punctuation?

- ○ "How long have you had this pain? asked Dr Chou.
- ○ "How long have you had this pain?" asked Dr Chou.
- ○ "How long have you had this pain," asked Dr Chou.
- ○ "How long have you had this pain." asked Dr Chou.

31. Which word makes this sentence make sense?

Martin likes to watch cartoons _____ he is eating his breakfast.

- ○ while
- ○ because
- ○ after
- ○ during

Shade two bubbles.

32. Where should the missing speech marks (" and ") go?

◯ ◯ ◯ ◯

Can I have a bag of chips please? said Thomas to the shopkeeper.

Shade one bubble.

33. Which word correctly completes the sentence?

Laila has _____ her project home.

took　　　　taking　　　　tooken　　　　taken

◯　　　　◯　　　　◯　　　　◯

34. Which word correctly completes the sentence?

I would like to buy _____ jumpers.

those　　　　that　　　　them　　　　this

◯　　　　◯　　　　◯　　　　◯

Read the text *Chinese on the Goldfields*. Choose the correct word to fit in each gap.

Shade one bubble.

Chinese on the Goldfields

When the Chinese arrived _____**35.**_____ the goldfields, they worked together in teams. Each

member took on duties. Some would cook _____**36.**_____ others would mine or grow vegetables.

Many white miners were annoyed _____**37.**_____ the Chinese worked in abandoned mines and found

gold. They also sent gold back _____**38.**_____ China.

_____**39.**_____ had a different culture and religion but the other miners did not understand this.

35. ◯ with　　　◯ in　　　◯ for　　　◯ at

36. ◯ because　　　◯ while　　　◯ but　　　◯ also

37. ◯ despite　　　◯ though　　　◯ because　　　◯ so

38. ◯ to　　　◯ for　　　◯ in　　　◯ at

39. ◯ Them　　　◯ We　　　◯ They　　　◯ You

Read the text *Earthquake*. Choose the correct word to fit in each gap.

Shade one bubble.

Earthquake

40. On January 12, 2010 a massive earthquake hit Haiti, the _____ nation in the western hemisphere.

  ○ poor   ○ poorly
  ○ poorer   ○ poorest

41. The earthquake, _____ 7.0 on the Richter scale, killed over a hundred thousand people.

○ measure   ○ measures
○ measured   ○ measuring

42. Which word makes this sentence correct?

Steve Smith dived full length to _____ the ball.

caught   catch   catching   catches
○   ○   ○   ○

43. Which word makes this sentence correct?

I will _____ your invitation to the birthday party.

expect   accept   except   excepted
○   ○   ○   ○

44. Which word or words makes this sentence correct?

Your dog, Ruby is lazy but my dog, Lucy is _____.

lazy   lazily   lazier   laziest
○   ○   ○   ○

Shade one bubble.

45. Which word describes how Brianna painted?

Brianna's painting of the (beautiful,) (green) countryside was (carefully) done.

46. Which of these sentences is a statement?

○ When are you buying a new car

○ When I get my new cricket bat you may use it

○ When is the soccer match being played

○ When are we having a barbecue

47. Which option completes the sentence correctly.

When you play softball all you need is _____ .

○ a softball bat, a softball and some bases

○ a softball bat a softball and some bases.

○ a softball bat a softball, and some bases.

○ a softball bat, a softball, and some bases.

48. Which word or words makes this sentence correct?

The police locked the bank down because there _____ .

○ had been a bank robbery   ○ is a bank robbery

○ might be a bank robbery   ○ should be a bank robbery

49. Where should you place the missing comma?

Unfortunately ↑ the gravel ↑ road was closed ↑ because of a nasty ↑ car accident.

    ○   ○   ○   ○

50. Which sentence uses the apostrophe (') correctly?

○ Both of Lisa's bikes needed to be repaired.

○ Both of lisa's bikes needed to be repaired.

○ Both of Lisas bike's needed to be repaired.

○ Both of lisas bike's needed to be repaired.

PRACTICE 5 ○ ○ ○

Penguin Fact Files

The Emperor Penguin is the largest of all penguins. They can be found on pack ice in Antarctica. These penguins keep themselves warm because they have a thick layer of blubber (fat) and shiny, waterproof feathers that insulate them from the cold.

Emperor Penguins may stand up to 1.1 metres tall and weigh up to 30 kilograms.

Emperor Penguins have large heads and short thick, necks. They have black bills with yellow-orange beaks. Their bodies are streamlined and they have short, wedge-shaped tails and tiny wings like flippers. They have black webbed feet, which help them to swim.

These creatures are carnivores, eating mainly fish and squid.

Rockhopper Penguins are small, crested penguins that can be aggressive. They are called "rockhoppers" because they tend to jump from rock to rock. Like most penguins they have waterproof, shiny

feathers that keep their skin dry. Rockhopper Penguins grow to around 55 centimetres tall and they weigh about 3 kilograms. Their bodies are streamlined. This allows them to move well in the water. They have big heads, short, thick necks, wedge-shaped tails and tiny wings like flippers. Like all penguins they have webbed feet, allowing them to swim well. On top of their heads they have a black and yellow droopy feathery crest, a bright orange-red bill and red eyes.

Being carnivores, their diet consists mainly of crustaceans and small fish.

The Gentoo penguin is a medium sized penguin. It grows to around 75-90cm and weighs about 5 kilograms. They have bright red-orange bills and conspicuous white eye patches which make them easy to identify.

They feed mainly on fish, krill and squid.

Read *Penguin Fact Files* and answer the questions.

1. The smallest penguin in this text is the

○ Emperor Penguin. ○ Rockhopper Penguin. ○ Gentoo Penguin. ○ Adelie Penguin.

2. This text

○ explains how penguins find food. ○ gives information about some penguins.

○ gives information about 3 Australian penguins. ○ is a story about penguins.

3. Penguins have waterproof feathers to

○ help them catch food. ○ swim well.

○ camouflage them from predators. ○ keep them warm and dry.

4. The penguins in this text are all

○ the same height. ○ the same weight. ○ carnivores. ○ hungry.

5. It is easy to recognise a Gentoo penguin because

○ it is medium-sized. ○ it has white patches near the eyes.

○ it doesn't have webbed feet. ○ it has a bright red-orange bill.

6. The word "streamlined" means

○ a narrow river. ○ efficient. ○ in a line. ○ floating.

COUNCIL CITY WASTE
3 – Bin Waste Service

Kitchen Tidy Bin

To collect food waste in the kitchen and transport to the Organics bin.

Organics Bin

✓ All food waste
✓ Grass clippings
✓ Weeds, leaves and flowers
✓ Sticks and twigs
✓ Paper towel and tissues
✓ Pet excrement (wrapped in paper)
✗ **No plastic bags**

Recycling Bin

✓ Paper and cardboard
✓ Glass bottles and jars
✓ Cans and cartons
✓ Plastic bottles, tubs and jars (excluding bottle lids)
✓ Steel and aluminium cans
✓ Empty aerosol cans
✗ **No plastic bags**

Residual Garbage Bin

✓ Plastic bags, wrap and film
✓ Disposable nappies
✓ Personal hygiene and medical waste
✓ Polystyrene foam boxes and trays
✓ Potato chip and snack bags
✓ Pet excrement in plastic bags

Your **Organics** bin is collected weekly

Your **Recycling** bin is collected fortnightly highlighted in Yellow

Your **Residual Garbage** bin is collected fortnightly as highlighted in Red

AUGUST SEPTEMBER OCTOBER NOVEMBER DECEMBER
JANUARY FEBRUARY MARCH APRIL MAY JUNE

Read *Your Waste Bin Service* and answer the questions.

1. This text is probably

○ a procedure.   ○ a recount.   ○ an explanation.   ○ a discussion.

2. The main purpose of this text is to

○ show that there are three different coloured bins.   ○ give us a yearly calendar.

○ tell us what waste we should put in each bin.   ○ stop people from dumping waste.

3. The recycling bin is collected

○ every day.   ○ once a week.   ○ once every two weeks.   ○ once a month.

4. The organics bin is probably collected weekly because

○ the bin will smell badly if left for longer than a week.   ○ people waste lots of food.

○ the organics bin is smaller.   ○ the bin is very heavy.

5. An empty can of baked beans should be placed in the

○ Kitchen Tidy Bin.   ○ Organics Bin.   ○ Recycling Bin.   ○ Residual Garbage Bin.

6. Plastic bags need to be placed in the Residual Garbage Bin because they

○ cannot be re-used.   ○ cannot be recycled.

○ are organic.   ○ belong in the Kitchen Tidy Bin.

7. Bottle lids should probably be placed in the

○ Organics Bin.   ○ Recycling Bin.   ○ Residual Garbage Bin.   ○ Kitchen Tidy Bin.

The Shoes of Time

Matt and his mother, Jill had just moved to Hill End, a little country town near Bathurst after Matt's parents divorced. Matt and Jill were preparing to start a new life.

The old miner's hut they had moved to was just right. It had two bedrooms, a kitchen, a bathroom and a lounge room. Dust lay about the place like thick carpet and Matt coughed profusely as he entered the hut.

Although sad about his parents splitting up, Matt was excited about their new adventure and he dashed excitedly to his new bedroom. His bright blue eyes scanned the room and in the dim light he could make out a rickety, old mirror on the wall, his bed, which had been delivered that day and an old timber wardrobe that looked like it was ready for the dump.

Matt unpacked his suitcase and began to put his clothes into the wardrobe. He hung up the shirts that he would need for the long, humid summer months. His shorts and jeans were placed neatly into some of the drawers. As he went to put his socks into the last drawer he noticed that it was not empty.

In amongst the cobwebs in the drawer was a pair of old miner's boots. Matt screwed his face up when he saw how dirty they were. They were long, black wellington boots that went up to the knees of a grown man. But Matt was just eleven years old and these boots could have covered the length of his legs. Dried, crusty, century-old mud caked the boots and Matt was reluctant to pick them up.

Matt had heard stories about the gold rushes of the 1850s in school. Now he imagined a gold digger putting on these boots and walking outside to his claim, digging and cradling for hours without any reward for his work.

Matt smiled to himself and sat down to put the boots on. They looked way too big for him but amazingly; when he stood up they seemed to fit perfectly. Matt strode uneasily out of the room to show his Mum.

Matt could not find her. He walked through every room, which now seemed much cleaner and lived in than before. There seemed to be items in the rooms he had not seen before and he certainly hadn't seen the mining equipment by the door.

Matt walked out into the dusty, hot dirt track and he could not believe the sight before him. People came rushing by pushing old carts; others walked carrying large packs on their backs. Whole families were riding past in horses and carts carrying their worldly belongings. Small groups of Chinese men moved quickly here and there.

Something strange had happened! This was not the country town he had arrived at. Matt looked down at his boots and scratched his head.

Read *The Shoes of Time* and answer the questions.

1. This text is

◯ a factual recount.　◯ a narrative.　◯ an explanation.　◯ an information report.

2. Matt and his mother, Jill probably moved to Hill End to

◯ make a new start.　　　　　◯ get away from Matt's father.

◯ learn more about the gold rushes.　◯ find their fortune on the goldfields.

3. The old miner's hut was

◯ clean and bright.　◯ small and old.　◯ small, old and dirty.　◯ old but clean.

4. *"...he could make out a rickety old mirror on the wall,.."* Rickety probably means

◯ strong.　　◯ solid.　　◯ ancient.　　◯ about to collapse.

5. Matt *"sat down to put the boots on."* because

◯ he was too tired to stand up.　　◯ it was more difficult to put them on standing up.

◯ he didn't want to get dirty.　　◯ he didn't want to dirty the carpet.

6. *"Matt smiled to himself..."* because

◯ he looked silly wearing the boots.

◯ he remembered happy times with his family.

◯ he was thinking about his old school.

◯ he was imagining what it was like to be a digger on the goldfields.

POCKET MONEY SHOULD BE EARNED.

Do you agree?

What do you think of this statement? Write a text to convince the audience of your opinions. Think about:

- whether you agree, disagree or see both sides of the argument
- an introduction – introduce ideas by clearly saying what you think about the topic
- your arguments – give reasons or evidence to explain
- a conclusion – give a summary of the main points of your argument

Remember to

- plan your writing
- write in good sentences
- pay attention to spelling and punctuation
- choose words carefully to convince the audience of your opinions
- use a new paragraph when writing about a new idea
- edit your writing so that it makes sense

PRACTICE 6

The spelling mistake in each sentence has been circled. In the box next to each question, write the correct spelling for each circled word.

1. She made a (complaynt) about the boy's behaviour.

2. It is a great honour to (recive) this award.

3. David will (attemt) to complete the bike jump.

4. Mum used the (matereal) to make a dress.

5. Make sure that you (inclose) a stamped self-addressed envelope.

6. I was the art monitor in Jenny's (absense).

7. I (intind) to go to the rock concert on Sunday.

8. Christmas is a very (speshal) celebration for Christian people.

The spelling mistakes in these labels have been circled. In the box next to each question, write the correct spelling for each circled word.

Berry Beetroot Smoothie

INGREDIENTS

9. 1 cup of (slised) canned beetroot

10. (Harf) cup of whole strawberries

11. 1 cup of (rasberries)

Blend until smooth and enjoy!

12. 1 1/2 cups of apple (juse)

Each of these sentences has one word that is incorrect. In the box next to each question, write the correct spelling for each circled word.

13. Tania won many races because she was very (atheletic.)

14. My Dad decided to (leese) a car.

15. The car has (autermatic) transmission.

16. I have made the (desission) to play cricket this summer.

Each of these sentences has one word that is incorrect. In the box next to each question, write the correct spelling for each circled word.

17. My coach decided to (appoynt) me as captain of the team.

18. Our school's swimming carnival is an (annuel) event.

19. I am going to (prepair) for exams by studying hard.

20. I (sincerly) hope that you find your lost dog.

21. There was water leaking from the washing (masheen.)

22. The basketballer can slam dunk from a great (hight.)

23. My uncle said that he could (repare) my bike.

24. I wish to become an Australian (citerzen.)

25. The new boy at our school lives on Darling (Avenyou.)

PRACTICE 6

Read the text *Mowing the Lawn*. Choose the correct words that fill the gaps in the text.

Shade one bubble. ✏️

Mowing the Lawn

26. Tayla wheeled out the lawn mower

and _____ to mow

the lawn.

- ○ begin
- ○ begins
- ○ began
- ○ beginning

27. Shortly after she started,

the mower coughed, spluttered

and _____.

- ○ dying
- ○ dies
- ○ died
- ○ dying

28. _____ had only run

out of petrol.

- ○ Fortunately, she
- ○ Fortunately, you
- ○ Fortunately, they
- ○ Fortunately, it

Shade one bubble. ✏️

29. Which sentence contains the correct punctuation?

- ○ Would you like a cup of coffee.
- ○ What a beautiful bunch of flowers!
- ○ How are you feeling today.
- ○ Fold the paper carefully in half?

30. Which sentence contains the correct punctuation?

- ○ "Eggs, butter, sugar and flour is needed to bake a cake?" said the teacher
- ○ "Eggs, butter, sugar and flour is needed to bake a cake," said the teacher.
- ○ "Eggs, butter, sugar, and flour is needed to bake a cake," said the teacher.
- ○ "Eggs, butter, sugar and flour is needed to bake a cake!" said the teacher.

31. Which word makes this sentence make sense?

I will wash the dishes _____ we have eaten dinner.

- ○ during
- ○ before
- ○ while
- ○ after

Shade two bubbles.

32. Where should the missing speech marks (" and ") go?

○ Help me please! ○ cried the man ○ who had fallen down the stairs. ○

Shade one bubble.

33. Which word correctly completes the sentence?

I _____ a ferocious lion at the zoo.

saw   seen   sawn   seeing

○   ○   ○   ○

34. Which word correctly completes the sentence?

Barbara went to her sister's bedroom to see if she was _____.

wake   waking   awake   awoke

○   ○   ○   ○

Read the text *The Ball*. Choose the correct word to fit in each gap.

Shade one bubble.

The Ball

Princess Helena _____35._____ exceptionally beautiful at the ball. She had long, golden brown hair framed by a stunning tiara. The tiara was _____36._____ of solid gold and laced with jewels of different kinds.

_____37._____ long dress was of green silk made from China. Around her neck she _____38._____ a string of amazing white pearls.

The people gasped as she entered the ballroom. Then _____39._____ clapped as she took the hand of the Prince.

35. ○ look   ○ looks   ○ looked   ○ looking

36. ○ makes   ○ made   ○ make   ○ making

37. ○ Her   ○ She   ○ My   ○ Hers

38. ○ wearing   ○ wears   ○ wear   ○ wore

39. ○ he   ○ they   ○ she   ○ you

Read the text *Collision*. Choose the correct word to fit in each gap.

Shade one bubble.

Collision

40. An anti-whaling protest speedboat was _____ by a Japanese whaling ship in the Southern Ocean.

- ○ ram
- ○ rams
- ○ rammed
- ○ ramming

41. The speedboat named the "Ady Gil' was severely _____ but all six crew were rescued.

- ○ damaged
- ○ damages
- ○ damaging
- ○ damage

42. Which word makes this sentence correct?

Last year, Alice _____ an award-winning outfit.

design	designer	designs	designed
○	○	○	○

43. Which word makes this sentence correct?

Farah had a shower and _____ got dressed up.

so	later	now	after
○	○	○	○

44. Which word or words makes this sentence correct?

Although this month was wet, last month's weather was the _____ on record.

wetter	wettest	wetting	wet
○	○	○	○

Shade one bubble.

45. Which word describes how Maria felt about the roller coaster?

Maria's heart (raced) as she (worried) about the (speedy) twists and turns of the Demon ride.

46. Which of these sentences is a command?

◯ Please come here

◯ Why are you pushing him

◯ Get out of my house

◯ That's a really cool car

47. Which option completes the sentence correctly.

The pie contained _____ .

◯ beef, cheese and bacon.

◯ beef cheese, and bacon.

◯ beef, cheese and, bacon.

◯ beef cheese and bacon.

48. Which word or words makes this sentence correct?

Tom and Lana were very tired because they _____ .

◯ are bushwalking   ◯ were going bushwalking

◯ had been bushwalking   ◯ would be bushwalking

49. Where should you place the missing comma?

Unless ↑ a rule is introduced ↑ to stop injuries ↑ on the swings ↑ some children will get hurt.

◯   ◯   ◯   ◯

50. Which sentence uses the apostrophe (') correctly?

◯ Dad's golf clubs were stolen from the boot of the car.

◯ Dads' golf clubs were stolen from the boot of the car.

◯ Dads golf club's were stolen from the boot of the car.

◯ dads' golf clubs were stolen from the boot of the car.

Make a Lemon Battery

Aim: To make a small amount of electricity by making a lemon battery.

Equipment:
  1 fresh lemon
  1 twenty-cent piece
  1 old penny or two cent piece
  1 sharp knife

Procedure:
  1. Shake the lemon and roll it on a table. This will activate the juices.
  2. Ask an adult to help you cut two small slices in the lemon about 2.5 centimetres apart.
  3. Place the twenty-cent piece into one slice and the old penny or two cent piece into the other slice.
  4. At the same time touch both coins with your tongue. What do you feel? Is it a tingling sensation?

How it works:

The two coins are made of different metals and the acid in the lemon reacts differently with each coin. One coin gives off a positive charge while the other gives off a negative charge. These charges create a current, which flows if the battery circuit is complete.

Your tongue acts like a wire to make the circuit complete. This means that a small amount of electricity flows causing the tingling sensation on your tongue!

Read *Make a Lemon Battery* and answer the questions.

1. This text is

  ○ a procedure.   ○ an explanation.   ○ a procedure and an explanation.   ○ a recount.

2. The lemon needs to be shaken and rolled to

  ○ make the juices sour.   ○ get the juices flowing.

  ○ move the seeds.   ○ make it easy to cut.

3. The lemon needs to be fresh because it

  ○ will have a sweeter taste.   ○ will have a brighter yellow colour.

  ○ will be juicier.   ○ will smell if it is stale.

4. The purpose of the text is to

  ○ create electricity by making a lemon battery.   ○ complete an experiment safely.

  ○ cause a tingling sensation on your tongue.   ○ explain why we need batteries.

5. An adult is required to

  ○ cheer you on.   ○ cut the lemon.

  ○ provide the electricity.   ○ provide the coins.

6. Touching a coin with your tongue will cause

  ○ the coin to tingle.   ○ electricity to flow.   ○ nothing to happen.   ○ pain.

Was That Santa?

It was Christmas Eve and 10-year-old Nikki was excited about receiving her presents. The one thing Nikki most wanted was to actually see Santa. She tried to stay awake for his arrival.

The old green armchair was not exactly a bed but it was comfortable enough. Besides, she wanted to see Santa. Tahnee and Lisa said that he did not exist and Nikki was determined to prove them wrong.

She shifted uneasily as sleep drifted ever closer. Nikki had crept down from her bedroom after her parents and Tim; her younger brother had gone to bed. Now, here she lay in her pink bunny pyjamas on the armchair, covered in a blanket. Her tangled, blonde hair fell over her face, covering her eyes.

Just at that magical time between being asleep and awake she was jolted from her slumber by a loud thud. She sprang upright with her purple, woollen blanket covering her nose and her piercing blue eyes peering into the darkness. A cold shiver ran down her spine as she waited in anticipation.

Slow, deliberate footsteps moved in her direction. Nikki sat staring at the beautifully decorated Christmas tree in front of her, expecting at any moment to see Santa arriving with his heavily laden sack.

A large, dark shadow appeared in the doorway and a voice mumbled as it shuffled across, past the fireplace and straight towards a plate of cookies and a glass of milk.

Nikki's eyes widened.

'You're real!" she exclaimed. "I knew you were real."

The dark shadow turned around, startled. Nikki marvelled at his bright, red coat and enormous black boots, both of which seemed to be illuminated. He winked and smiled at her and put a finger to his mouth.

"You're supposed to be asleep young lady," he cried with a twinkle in his eye.

Nikki hung her head in shame.

"Actually, I'm glad you are awake," he continued. "I have a big problem you can help me with. I can't fit down the chimneys as I've eaten too much."

Read *Was That Santa?* and answer the questions.

1. Nikki stayed awake to see Santa because she
   - ○ had never seen him before.
   - ○ believed in Santa.
   - ○ wanted to prove that he existed.
   - ○ was not tired.

2. *"Just at that magical time between asleep and awake…"* This tells us that Nikki was
   - ○ fast asleep. ○ wide awake. ○ waiting for Santa. ○ dozing.

3. The loud thud made Nikki
   - ○ frightened. ○ hide. ○ sit up. ○ scream.

4. The author wants you to believe that
   - ○ children should try to wait up for Santa. ○ Santa is real.
   - ○ it is not easy being Santa. ○ Santa only has cookies and milk.

5. *"You're supposed to be asleep young lady,"…* This suggests that Santa was probably
   - ○ worried. ○ angry. ○ teasing her. ○ happy.

6. *"…his bright, red coat and enormous black boots both of which seemed to be illuminated.* Illuminated probably means
   - ○ like a lemon. ○ colourful. ○ wet. ○ bright and shining.

7. To help Santa, Nikki will probably have to
   - ○ pull the sleigh. ○ eat the cookies and drink the milk.
   - ○ help him get back on his sleigh. ○ help deliver presents.

The Trial of Goldilocks

After entering the house of the Three Bears, eating their porridge and breaking a chair, Goldilocks was arrested at her cottage on the edge of the forest. She faced a court hearing.

Judge:	Goldilocks, you have been charged with breaking and entering and wilful destruction of property. How do you plead?
Goldilocks:	Not guilty, Your Honour.
Judge:	Lawyer, please call your first witness to the stand.
Lawyer:	I call Father Bear to the stand. *(Father Bear takes the stand.)* Father Bear, what happened on the morning that the alleged crime was committed?
Father Bear:	My wife, my son and I decided to go for a walk because the porridge that Mother Bear had made was too hot. We thought that we might be able to find some nice berries or some honey to add to the porridge.
Judge:	What did you notice when you returned home?
Father Bear:	The house was a mess! Mother Bear and I always keep the house neat and tidy but there was spilt porridge on the table and the floor. The spoons had been dropped on the floor and I was very upset.
Lawyer:	Thank you, Father Bear. You may stand down. *(Father Bear leaves the stand.)* I now call Mother Bear to the stand. *(Mother Bear takes the stand.)* Mother Bear, what else did you see after you came back to your cottage?
Mother Bear:	Oh, it was terrible! I was so upset that I cried. Our beautiful chairs had been ruined. Father Bear's chair and my chair had been totally ruined with mud. I'm sure that Goldilocks must have been rolling in mud before she entered the house. Then, to make matters worse, my poor Baby Bear's chair was in pieces. We saved up so much money for that chair! I think that Goldilocks needs to go on a diet!
Lawyer:	Thank you, Mother Bear. You may stand down. *(Mother Bear leaves the stand.)* I now call Baby Bear to the stand. *(Baby Bear takes the stand.)* Baby Bear, can you add any other information?
Baby Bear: (pointing)	She was sleeping in my bed! That was my bed!
Lawyer:	What did you do when she woke up?
Baby Bear:	She screamed and ran out of the house. We called the Police straight away.
Lawyer:	Thank you, Baby Bear. You may stand down. *(Baby Bear leaves the stand.)* I now call Goldilocks to the stand. *(Goldilocks takes the stand.)* Goldilocks, the Three Bears have given us compelling evidence about the crime. What do you have to say?
Goldilocks:	I didn't do it! I was home baking cookies for my Grandma!
Lawyer:	The Forensic Police have your fingerprints on the door of the cottage and your muddy footprints inside the house, which are the same size as yours. What do you say about that?

Read *The Trial of Goldilocks* and answer questions

1. Goldilocks' cottage is

⬭ next door to the Bears.

⬭ in the city.

⬭ in the forest.

⬭ at the edge of the forest.

2. Goldilocks was probably arrested by the

⬭ Police.

⬭ Lawyer.

⬭ Judge.

⬭ Fire Brigade.

3. Baby Bear's chair was probably

⬭ not well made.

⬭ cheap.

⬭ expensive.

⬭ very old.

4. The purpose of the text is to

⬭ tell an old story in a different way for older readers.

⬭ explain that Goldilocks is not a hero.

⬭ send Goldilocks to jail.

⬭ give information about Goldilocks' family.

5. Mother Bear suggested that Goldilocks go on a diet because she

⬭ ate three bowls of porridge.

⬭ baked cookies for Grandma.

⬭ is always hungry.

⬭ sat on Baby Bear's chair and broke it.

6. The job of keeping the house clean belongs to

⬭ Mother Bear.

⬭ Mother Bear and Father Bear.

⬭ Father Bear.

⬭ The Three Bears.

7. The evidence that the Police found was

⬭ spilt porridge on the table.

⬭ a broken chair.

⬭ fingerprints and footprints.

⬭ muddy chairs.

THE FLOOD

You are going to write a story or narrative The idea for your story is "The Flood".

- Where did this happen?
- Who was there?
- What happened?
- How did they survive?
- What damage was done?

Remember to

- plan your writing before you begin
- write in good sentences
- pay attention to spelling and punctuation
- choose words carefully
- use a new paragraph when writing about a new idea
- edit your writing so that it makes sense

PRACTICE 1

LANGUAGE CONVENTIONS
1. family 2. friends 3. insects 4. flood 5. search 6. angry 7. through 8. proud 9. water bottle 10. reflector 11. pedal 12. tyre 13. surprise 14. destroy 15. concert 16. listen 17. motor 18. remember 19. different 20. complete 21. introduce 22. balloons 23. commence 24. Sometimes 25. dangerous 26. her 27. they 28. Finally, Helen 29. What is the time now in England? 30. "May I borrow your pencil?" asked Minh. 31. Although 32. "What a fantastic goal" 33. shaken or shaking 34. saw 35. these 36. near 37. through 38. its 39. eat 40. quickly 41. were 42. brought 43. Whose 44. the fastest 45. neatly 46. How will you travel to the city? 47. apples, grapes and bananas 48. rain had fallen 49. work, 50. Tony's friends like to play with cricket bats.

READING
Born to Fly 1. 1745. 2. hot air 3. tied down. 4. Lyons. 5. The wind. 6. A rooster, a duck and a sheep.
First Man on the Moon 1. Neil Armstrong. 2. July 20, 1969. 3. there is less gravity on the moon. 4. provides oxygen and controls the temperature and pressure inside the suit. 5. see what they are made up of. 6. a factual recount.
Every Drop Counts 1. encourage people to use less water. 2. it is not as hot at these times so less water gets evaporated. 3. some pipes might leak, which means you waste more water. 4. we should monitor our use of water. 5. water gets wasted and ends up in our rivers. 6. each person must take responsibility for saving water.

WRITING – Marooned on an Island
Teacher to check

PRACTICE 2

LANGUAGE CONVENTIONS
1. answer 2. meant 3. truly 4. straight 5. doctor 6. minute 7. enough 8. business 9. fir 10. pointed 11. claws 12. limbs 13. February 14. Instead 15. teacher 16. themselves 17. Christmas 18. restrain 19. justice 20. stopped 21. objection 22. gentleman 23. supply 24. pleasure 25. direction 26. his 27. him 28. Carefully, he 29. What a fantastic catch! 30. "Have you seen my car keys?" asked Dad. 31. While 32. "I think I saw a ghost!" 33. crying 34. hidden 35. from 36. in 37. known 38. Besides Earth, 39. which 40. tightly 41. They 42. couldn't 43. Which 44. the silliest 45. burning 46. When will you travel to the city? 47. books, pens and pencils 48. had been playing in the mud 49. injured, 50. We had seen Trinh's books in the library.

READING
Australian Lizards 1. Goanna. 2. Boyd's Forest Dragon and the Frilled Neck Lizard. 3. are native to Australia. 4. protect themselves in some way. 5. give information about some Australian lizards. 6. school students.
The Jungle 1. a lion. 2. overhead. 3. a boy's imagination. 4. he was in a hurry to find the lion. 5. it was time for dinner. 6. Tom ran out the back door. The monkeys teased Tom. A pair of toucans frightened Tom. Tom went inside the house to have dinner.
Which is Better? Summer or Winter? 1. To find out which season was better. 2. To get readers to think carefully about the topic. 3. Hanging our clothes outside on the clothes line. 4. Convince people that summer is the better season. 5. Being environmentally friendly. 6. The clocks are put forward an hour.

WRITING – Attack of the Tarantulas
Teacher to check

PRACTICE 3

LANGUAGE CONVENTIONS
1. trouble 2. women 3. Wednesday 4. grammar 5. often 6. piece 7. could 8. hoarse 9. vapour 10. dries 11. clouds 12. ocean 13. guess 14. though 15. assist 16. sudden 17. organise 18. forward 19. personal 20. prompt 21. summon 22. vacation 23. statement 24. refer 25. importance 26. them 27. them 28. Swiftly, they 29. How wonderful your picture is! 30. "Will you be attending the excursion?" asked the teacher. 31. During 32. "I did not rob the jewellery store!" 33. frozen 34. did 35. this 36. its 37. feeds 38. these 39. to 40. slowly 41. They 42. beaten 43. whom 44. the funniest 45. calmly 46. What a beautiful bunch of flowers! 47. a tuna sandwich, an apple and a drink. 48. had been in hospital 49. daily, 50. Harry's crayons had been taken from his bag.

READING
Sammy Spy – Kid Detective 1. a narrative. 2. they were the lunch monitors that day. 3. that his eyesight is very good. 4. a small piece of egg. 5. he wanted to smell their breath. 6. a dog.
How to Make a Cork Boat 1. a procedure. 2. cut the cork. 3. as a mast. 4. cut in half with a pair of scissors. 5. show people how to make a simple boat out of cork. 6. the bath tub. 7. make different types of boats with the materials.
The Glow 1. a space ship. 2. surge 3. he could sense that something was going to happen. 4. he was hot. 5. the silver walkway. 6. A silver disc landed in Simon's front yard. A hazy glow filled the room. Simon's heart was beating hard. A creature waddled out of the disc.

Writing – The Internet is a Good Thing
Teacher to check

PRACTICE 4

LANGUAGE CONVENTIONS
1. where 2. raise 3. cough 4. ache 5. built 6. believe 7. could 8. among 9. planted 10. grow 11. basket 12. vegetables 13. sugar 14. loose 15. imprison 16. earliest 17. entertain 18. difficulty 19. support 20. salary 21. scene 22. convict 23. wreck 24. Finally 25. debate 26. have 27. this 28. Unfortunately, they 29. My name is Albert John Farmer 30. "John Oxley was a famous Australian explorer," stated the teacher. 31. Due 32. "Such is life." 33. shook 34. likes 35. has 36. because 37. it 38. feeds 39. grips 40. stretched 41. heavier 42. bought 43. whose 44. easiest 45. lovingly 46. What I need is a hammer and nails. 47. cheese, tomato and onion 48. was hungry 49. Recently, 50. All of the students' projects were destroyed in the fire.

READING
Hargraves Finds Gold 1. 1851. 2. he knew the terrain there was similar to California. 3. because Edward Hargraves taught them. 4. They could find gold in Australia 5. Recount the first gold discoveries in Australia and how the country grew. 6. Many new towns and transport links to be developed.

The Australian Flag 1. September 1901. 2. The flags of St George, St Andrew and St Patrick. 3. five people. 4. it shows our place in the world. 5. explain how the Australian flag was designed and what it means. 6. Many people don't know the meaning behind the Australian flag.

Our Camp at Milson Island 1. more than two hours 2. experience new ways to have fun outside. 3. he probably doesn't like heights. 4. he had to walk up the hill carrying his heavy bag. 5. recount the trip to camp. 6. hot dogs.

WRITING – Today's Children are Couch Potatoes
Teacher to check

PRACTICE 5

LANGUAGE CONVENTIONS
1. beginning 2. whether 3. their 4. separate 5. Since 6. wear 7. laid 8. lose 9. glass 10. rinse 11. emptied 12. sure 13. Tuesday 14. coming 15. prefer 16. issue 17. publish 18. director 19. estate 20. injure 21. unfortunate 22. primary 23. elaborate 24. contract 25. express 26. ridden 27. cried 28. Luckily 29. Don't ever do that again! 30. "How long have you had this pain?" asked Dr Chou. 31. While 32. "Can I have a bag of chips please," 33. taken 34. those 35. at 36. while 37. because 38. to 39. They 40. poorest 41. measuring 42. catch 43. accept 44. lazier 45. carefully 46. When I get my new cricket bat you may use it. 47. A softball bat, a softball and some bases. 48. had been a bank robbery 49. Unfortunately, 50. Both of Lisa's bikes needed to be repaired.

READING
Penguin Fact Files 1. Rockhopper Penguin. 2. gives information about some penguins. 3. keep them warm and dry. 4. carnivores. 5. it has white patches near the eyes. 6. efficient.

3 – Bin Waste Service 1. an explanation. 2. tell us what waste we should put in each bin. 3. once every two weeks. 4. the bin will smell badly if left for longer than a week. 5. Recycling bin. 6. cannot be recycled. 7. Residual Garbage Bin.

The Shoes of Time 1. a narrative. 2. make a new start. 3. small, old and dirty. 4. about to collapse. 5. it was more difficult to put them on standing up. 6. he was imagining what it was like to be a digger on the goldfields.

WRITING – Pocket Money Should Be Earned Teacher to check

PRACTICE 6

LANGUAGE CONVENTIONS
1. complaint 2. receive 3. attempt 4. material 5. enclose 6. absence 7. intend 8. special 9. sliced 10. Half 11. raspberries 12. juice 13. athletic 14. lease 15. automatic 16. decision 17. appoint 18. annual 19. prepare 20. sincerely 21. machine 22. height 23. repair 24. citizen 25. Avenue 26. began 27. died 28. Fortunately, it 29. What a beautiful bunch of flowers! 30. "Eggs, butter, sugar and flower is needed to bake a cake," said the teacher. 31. after 32. "Help me please!" 33. saw 34. awake 35. looked 36. made 37. Her 38. wore 39. they 40. rammed 41. damaged 42. designed 43. later 44. wettest 45. worried 46. Get out of my house! 47. beef, cheese and bacon 48. had been bushwalking 49. swings, 50. Dad's golf clubs were stolen from the boot of the car.

READING
Make a Lemon Battery 1. a procedure and an explanation. 2. get the juices flowing. 3. will be juicier. 4. create electricity by making a lemon battery. 5. cut the lemon. 6. electricity to flow.

Was That Santa? 1. wanted to prove that he existed. 2. dozing. 3. sit up. 4. Santa is real. 5. teasing her. 6. bright and shining. 7. help him get back to his sleigh.

The Trial of Goldilocks 1. at the edge of the forest. 2. Police. 3. expensive. 4. tell an old story in a different way for older readers. 5. sat on Baby Bear's Chair and broke it. 6. Mother Bear and Father Bear. 7. fingerprints and footprints.

WRITING – The Flood Teacher to check

	ITEMS IN NEED OF ATTENTION
Practice 1	
Language Conventions	
Reading	
Writing	
Practice 2	
Language Conventions	
Reading	
Writing	
Practice 3	
Language Conventions	
Reading	
Writing	

	ITEMS IN NEED OF ATTENTION
Practice 4	
Language Conventions	
Reading	
Writing	
Practice 5	
Language Conventions	
Reading	
Writing	
Practice 6	
Language Conventions	
Reading	
Writing	